The Important Early Years

Intelligence Through Movement Experiences

Liselott Diem
Kathi Walz, translator

A project of the
Association for Research, Administration,
Professional Councils and Societies
and the
Council on Physical Education for Children
of the National Association for
Sport and Physical Education
Associations of the
American Alliance for Health, Physical Education,
Recreation and Dance

Originally published as
Auf die ersten Lebensjahre kommt es an
© 1986 Meyer & Meyer Verlag, Aachen, Germany

We are indebted to Meyer & Meyer Verlag for use
of the illustrations from the German edition.

English translation © 1991
American Alliance for Health,
Physical Education, Recreation and Dance
1990 Association Drive, Reston, VA 22091

ISBN 0-88314-491-3

PURPOSES OF THE AMERICAN ALLIANCE FOR HEALTH, PHYSICAL EDUCATION, RECREATION AND DANCE

The American Alliance is an educational organization, structured for the purposes of supporting, encouraging, and providing assistance to member groups and their personnel throughout the nation as they seek to initiate, develop, and conduct programs in health, leisure, and movement-related activities for the enrichment of human life.

Alliance objectives include:

1. Professional growth and development—to support, encourage, and provide guidance in the development and conduct of programs in health, leisure, and movement-related activities which are based on the needs, interests, and inherent capacities of the individual in today's society.

2. Communication—to facilitate public and professional understanding and appreciation of the importance and value of health, leisure, and movement-related activities as they contribute toward human well-being.

3. Research—to encourage and facilitate research which will enrich the depth and scope of health, leisure, and movement-related activities, and to disseminate the findings to the profession and other interested and concerned publics.

4. Standards and guidelines—to further the continuous development and evaluation of standards within the profession for personnel and programs in health, leisure, and movement-related activities.

5. Public affairs—to coordinate and administer a planned program of professional, public, and governmental relations that will improve education in areas of health, leisure, and movement-related activities.

6. To conduct such other activities as shall be approved by the Board of Governors and the Alliance Assembly, provided that the Alliance shall not engage in any activity which would be inconsistent with the status of an educational and charitable organization as defined in Section 501(c)(3) of the Internal Revenue Code of 1954 or any successor provision thereto, and none of the said purposes shall at any time be deemed or construed to be purposes other than the public benefit purposes and objectives consistent with such educational and charitable status.

Bylaws, Article III

Contents

	Foreword	vi
	Introduction	vii
1	Learning During the Prenatal Period. A Mother-to-Be's Everyday Behavior Is Already Influencing the Child's Growth and Development. Fitness Training Before Pregnancy Prepares the Mother for Pregnancy.	1
2	Supporting the Movement Activities of a Newborn. Moving Along and Moving Alone. Bodily Contact as a Means of Communication.	4
3	Practical Examples for Joyful Play in the First Year of Life.	8
4	Refinement of Perception. Watching Moving Objects.	11
5	Standing Up Without Help. The Importance of the Crawling Stage. Unsupported Standing as Proof of Balance.	14
6	Promoting Spontaneity. Further Play With Fingers and Toes. Contact Play.	18
7	Coordination: Testing Balance, Responses. Variations of Accomplished Motor Skills. Orientation in Space.	21
8	Suppression of Movement Exploration Creates Handicaps. The Importance of Climbing Experiences and Gripping Efficiency. Gaining Strength Through Hanging and Swinging.	24
9	Learning Movement Patterns Through Active Participation and Imitation. Movement Perception.	28
10	Perceptual Learning. Numerous Variations in Perception. Activity With Balloons. Examples for the Distinction of Direction, Shape, Speed, and Space.	31
11	Sufficient Time for Play. Ability to Play Implies Concentration. Invitation to Play Is More Important Than Directed Play.	34
12	Sound and Movement. Monotonous Activities as Stepping Stones to Rhythmics. Development of an Individualized Expression of Sound.	37

13	Examples for Situational Learning Experiences. The "Infant Jumper," Sled Riding, and Swinging. The Learning of Complex Actions.	41
14	Sports Activities Requiring Balance: Riding a Scooter, Roller Skating, Bicycling, Ice Skating, and Snow Skiing.	44
15	Learning Through Problem Solving. Positive and Negative Aggressive Behavior. Self-Awareness Leading to Self-Confidence.	46
16	Imaginary and Creative Movement Ideas. Learning Through Discovery.	49
17	Play Activities and Play Concepts. Cooperation in Group Play.	53
18	Playing Together, Action and Interaction. Children Look for Companionship During Play. Partnership and Cooperation.	56
19	Development of Individuality and Self-Confidence. Small Groups and Play Units.	59
20	By Playing Together, Parents Achieve a Closer Relationship With Their Children.	61
21	Health Education. Children Are Endurance Achievers. Conditioning of the Body to Withstand Climatic Changes Need Not Be a Tough Task. Hygienic Measures.	64
22	Good Posture Is Not a Static Concept. Strength and Weakness of the Foot and Back. Control of Everyday Behavior.	66
23	Endurance and Speed.	70
24	Strength, Flexibility, and Skillfullness.	73
25	Properly Planned Play Areas in the Home, Near the Home, and on the Playground.	75
26	Appropriate Play Equipment.	79
27	Tests and Self-Evaluation of Movement Performance—0–5 Years.	82
28	Tests and Self-Evaluation—Examples for 6–8 Years.	87

Foreword

With the explosive interest in early childhood education throughout the United States as well as the world, the translation of this book from the German version to English is very timely.

Liselott Diem is one of the leading women in the physical education profession internationally. She held a professorship at the Deutsche Sporthochschule in Cologne, Germany until 1974 and even today still heads the Carl Diem Institute. She has conducted workshops and made many presentations worldwide, and her work with children is well known and highly regarded. She is a prolific author in the areas of preschool and elementary physical education. One of her earlier books, *Who Can*, published in 1955, was translated at George Williams College and distributed by the Alliance in 1977.

Liselott Diem has served on the board of the International Council on Health, Physical Education, and Recreation, has been president of the International Association of Physical Education and Sports for Girls and Women, and has been a member of the German Olympic Committee, as well as holding many other prestigious offices.

Readers will find the content of this book practical and stimulating as well as compatible with early childhood development theory and practice in the United States. Diem believes in setting the environment in such a way as to challenge the child rather than directing the child to play. She encourages learning by discovery, reinforcing of natural situations, learning by doing, and developing self-confidence and self-esteem through diverse movement experiences. The word "training" appears regularly in the translation but should not be threatening to the reader who examines the complete text carefully. One will find that the author capitalizes on the instinctive play of children to explore and to learn to know about themselves and their world. At times, the reader may question the safety of some activities or suggested play equipment because of the constant threat of litigation in the United States. One needs to use judgment regarding their use in a local situation.

Content of the book covers prenatal through age eight with a heavy focus on preprimary years. Chapters include information on activities by age groupings. The book discusses development of motor skills as well as the development of the whole child cognitively and affectively. Profuse illustrations help to interpret the text.

This book is easy to read and useful for both the professional and the lay reader. It makes a significant contribution to the literature.

MARGIE R. HANSON
Vice President, AAHPERD, and
Consultant for Children's Programs

Introduction

"What little Hans doesn't learn now, big Hans will never learn at all." With slight modification, this old German proverb is being repeated in the more recent theory of learning. Early childhood experiences are the most important, that is, the impressions children gain from their environment, the encouragements or restrictions they will encounter, and the stimulating or limiting atmosphere within which they grow up. The development of our rational thinking, our attention span, and our ability to memorize in the very first years of life are very much dependent upon motor experiences in the true sense of the word—through exploring and comprehending. Perceptual movement awareness depends on appropriate action at the right time. As children's movements become more assured, they develop their own interests and keep their zest for learning alive.

Learning is based on experiences. Each advancement opens up new learning situations. Learning provides children with the means to prove themselves and to think and act on their own. These early learning experiences should never be forced upon the child; they should develop through self-discovery, play with others, and personal challenges. Uninhibited movement experiences, rather than regimented or forced activities, produce the essential and lasting curiosity and thirst for knowledge necessary for human creativity.

This book discusses the following:
• spontaneity and sureness of movement;
• keen perceptual awareness;
• orientation in space;
• rational visualization and creativity in movement;
• comprehension of situations and independent reaction.

The book provides a variety of suggestions on how to promote a child's own competence, starting in the very first year of life.

LISELOTT DIEM

About the Translation

Appreciation goes to Kathi Walz, professor emeritus, Kent State University, Kent, Ohio, for making this important German book available to English readers. A former student of Diem's, Kathi Walz consulted with her in the work of translation; she was assisted by Regina Walz Simpson and Heinrich Walz.

1 Learning During the Prenatal Period. A Mother-to-Be's Everyday Behavior Is Already Influencing the Child's Growth and Development. Fitness Training Before Pregnancy Prepares the Mother for Pregnancy.

One might think we are carrying things too far when we talk about "learning" during the prenatal period, but some studies indicate that the fetus is subjected to stimuli and can react to them, and consequently, the necessary prerequisites for learning are present. The prenatal life of the child, which has not been researched extensively, is increasingly arousing the interest of science. Not only genes, but also the general mood of the mother—whether she feels well or is irritated—have a direct impact on the condition of the child. This applies not only to the mother's nutrition, but also to the use of medication in any form.

The mother's state of physical activity and her degree of confidence while moving about are decisive factors in the development of the child. The mother-to-be's physical fitness and the way she moves directly affect the child.

Fitness training during pregnancy may be linked to three areas, each one dependent upon the other:
1. Training of the heart—circulatory and metabolic systems, respiratory and endurance training.
2. Training of the muscular system, especially the muscles of the foot, leg, abdomen, and back, since these body parts have to support additional weight as the body's condition undergoes changes. Related to this is the development of a refined sense of correct body alignment, allowing for conscious adjustment while the body's proportions are constantly changing. Mothers who are blessed with strong foot and leg muscles do not suffer from constriction of venal blood circulation and the resulting enlargement of the veins. They avoid standing

Starting with their first hour of life, newborns need close contact with an adult. They will learn through differentiated perception.

for long periods and relax and loosen up strained muscles at the right time.
3. Coordination training, which is the special training for developing balance, fast reactions, and skillfulness to safeguard against disturbances of equilibrium.

Mothers who feel physically fit are usually more efficient and therefore more in balance. For example, they feel that the increasing weight of the child is less troublesome and therefore move about with undiminished range of movement. Due to this unhampered range of movement, the fetus is exposed to stimuli and experiences with respect to change of speed as well as movement directions such as up, down, and sideways.

Fitness is always a comprehensive term—comprised not only of strength, but also the necessary adaptability. The ability to rest and relax can be practiced systematically. According to Read [an M.D. from England], this leads to a less painful birth, since stressed and tense behavior will intensify the pain. The pregnancy period as the prelude to birth and the life of a child entails not only a versatile physical training by the mother, but also sound knowledge of the changes occurring in bodily functions. This knowledge helps ease the mother-to-be's mind at the appropriate moment since the well-trained woman is "very much aware" of the changes occurring in her body and its functions. She also learns to overcome weakness and disorders on her own.

Sports such as swimming, recreational ball games, running, hiking, and mountain and stair climbing can be practiced in moderation until the very last day of pregnancy. This enhances the vitality of both mother and child. Children who are active before birth are leaning toward greater competency in motor and speech development after birth. Speech and motor development are dependent upon each other.

Some nations count the day of birth as completion of the first year of life. Consequently, the "first nine months of life" represent an important stage in the development of a child's personality. By the end of the first trimester, children have mastered quite a few skills: they can push with their legs, twist their feet, curl and spread apart their toes, make a fist, move their thumbs, bend their wrists, turn their heads, look cross-eyed, wrinkle their foreheads, open their mouths, and press their lips tightly together.

2 Supporting the Movement Activities of a Newborn. Moving Along and Moving Alone. Bodily Contact as a Means of Communication.

Newborns astonish observers with the intensity of their movement activities and the abundance of accomplished movement skills. They can stretch and bend fingers, feet, and knees. While lying in a prone position, they can draw their knees close to their stomachs, and, using their toes, they can push off strongly from the surface below. Fingers can so tightly grasp a rod that one is able to lift them off the ground.

From the very first day on, newborns try again and again to lift their heavy heads. Such attempts increase the strength of the back beyond that already in existence at birth. This is a prerequisite for a child's ability to rise up. Such activity further demonstrates that during the first days of life, the baby's prone position, as well as the lifting of the head, the drawing of the legs to the stomach, and the pushing off—even with the mother's help—are natural movement experiences. After children are born, and while awake, they should be allowed to practice intense, spontaneous movement; they should never be hampered by tight swaddling or restrictive clothing. Motor impairment in later life can be traced to restrictions present in the environment of early childhood. The newborn's first hours and days are most important.

During pregnancy, the fetus "moves along" with the mother, and during infancy, those motor activities are expanded. During waking hours the baby may be carried, lifted, or moved into different positions. In other cultures parents expose their newborns to the outdoor environment so that they instinctively perceive sounds, smells, and the entire living atmosphere. A rich melodic voice, differentiated sound intensity, different noises, as well as music, light, and color effects, in the early experience phase create a heretofore barely registered perceptual training.

Could it be possible that affections or aversions, perceptions of fear or anxiety, that develop later on are the result of the first impressions received in life?

The newborn needs close human contact. The newborn needs caressing and skin-to-skin contact, which reinforce the feeling of warmth and security, especially if these contacts are coupled with soothing, rhythmical, and rocking motions. For instance: a child rests atop an adult's body so that the child moves up and down as the chest rises and falls during rhythmical breathing. The child's position should be changed quite often.

A newborn feels particularly comfortable in water in a position that eases the child's weight and offers a familiar and enjoyable sensation of floating. Our experimental water testing of babies in the beginners' pool at water temperatures of 32 degrees Celsius (90 degrees Fahrenheit) proved successful over a period of eight years. During these sessions parents together with their two-month-old babies softly glide through the water. They learn to support the children in prone or supine positions. While in the water the children enjoy unrestricted freedom in striking out with wide leg and arm movements. Motion pictures support these new findings: babies in the second month of life already display fine-tuned coordination in their swim-like movements with fully extended legs.

A baby's inborn swim-like movements have been analyzed by several scientists. Because of the similarity, these movements are also defined as stepping motions. For instance, if children are placed on their feet and are supported under their arms, they will move forward with walk-like steps. While moving, the flexible, gripping toes feel for a foothold. This wonderful toe gripping action and flexion of the foot, both of which are so functional in the first days of life, become dormant with lack of practice. The neuromuscular motor system is already developed at birth and constantly needs new and challenging stimuli. This stimuli/reaction system, so important for movement efficiency, can be compared to a widely dispersed telephone network, which increases its direct connections through differentiated circuitry—so, too, children become more efficient in their motor movements. On the other hand, unused wires are subject to corrosion and deterioration. Children then appear clumsy, stiff, or slow in their reactions. Consequently, inadequate motor coordination in an otherwise healthy child can be attributed to a lack of timely practice.

The gripping and supporting reactions of the hands and feet also require our help and stimulation. Children can take off from a springy mattress by pushing off with their

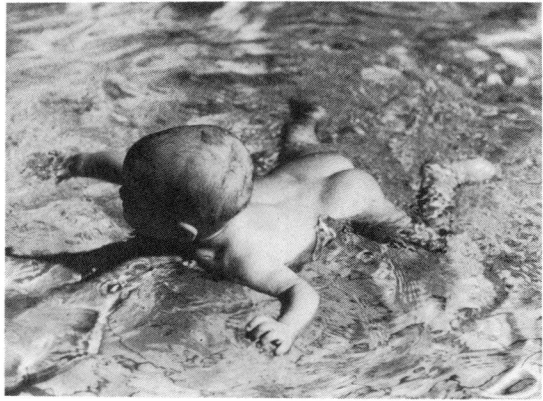

In a bathtub or in a warm swimming pool, children learn to move forward while being carefully supported by the fan-like, wide-spread hand of an adult. From moving along, children advance to moving alone.

Already in their first hours of life, healthy newborns try to lift their heads and display intense movement activity.

feet; they practice their jumping skills provided we lend our support. Held in a head-down position, children support themselves with their hands; they push and grip firmly with their fingers and toes, practicing manual dexterity with fingers and feet as long as we can coax them into it.

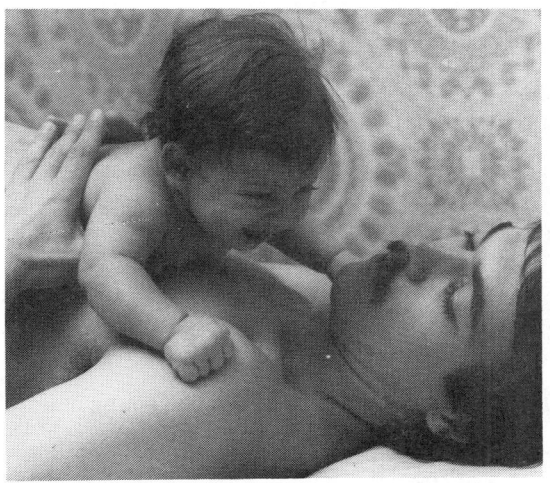

While lying on the father's chest, the baby feels the contact of his warm skin and his rhythmical breathing. These simultaneous movements can systematically be increased and thus refine the senses and movement instincts of a child.

3 Practical Examples for Joyful Play in the First Year of Life.

Parents should plan systematic exercises with the child. These should be five to ten minutes in duration, two to three times a day. What is important is the positive response of the child—exercising should be fun. Children slowly learn to react on their own. Smiling is a sure sign that a child is content, a sure sign of well-being in response to planned and carefully selected play interaction with their parents. We have to handle newborns with sympathetic understanding, with calm and unhurried movements, and with gentle hands that touch them warmly and delicately.

Following are examples of exercises for the young child.

Toe Gripping Exercise

While the child is lying in a supine position, carefully take hold of the lower leg with one hand and gently stroke across the sole of the foot with a finger of the other hand. The child will react by curling the toes. Use this reaction to rhythmically alternate between having your fingers grasped by the toes and then released and again stroking the soles of the feet with your finger. This creates a rhythmical pattern of bending and stretching. Repeat this play and observe the child's reaction. Be sure to switch feet during this play with the toes. Stroke and massage both feet gently and evenly in this manner so that the child constantly practices these toe gripping actions. Continue these stroking movements and move from the lower leg upward to the upper thigh. With both hands, take hold of both lower legs with the thumbs placed alongside each tibia bone. Now move the child's legs in rhythmical bicycle fashion—up, down, and around. In this bending and stretching exercise, the pattern can be changed by making the circular motion smaller or larger. To add variation to this toe gripping as well as leg bending and stretching play, change the tempo of the exercise.

Finger Grasping Exercises

If you touch a child's palm, the infant will strongly grasp your finger. Continue to use various stroking movements

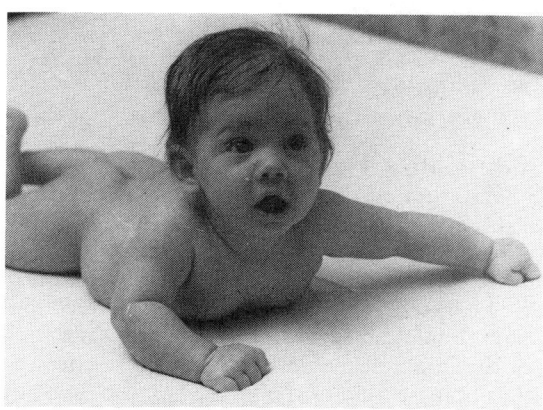

During the third and fourth months, children learn to support themselves securely on their hands. At first they clench their hands in a fist, then gradually open them, using fingers for support.

along the child's fingers. Watch closely for the child's reaction so that such activity turns into an interplay between action and reaction. Alternate between the child's left and right hands, but move on slowly to include the whole hand as well as the lower and upper arm. Let the child hold on to one of your fingers. At the same time, move both arms of the child in a circular pattern—upward, outward, downward. Change these circles by making them wider or

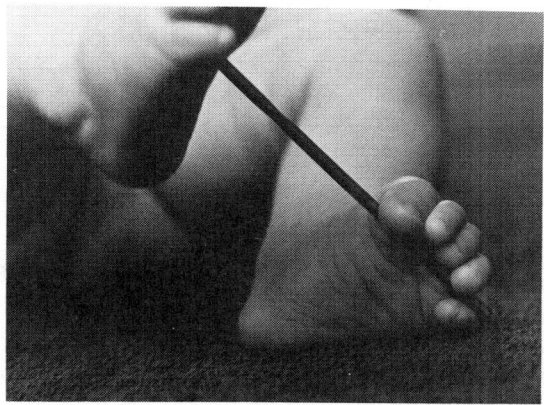

The toes of the newborn can spread and grip quite well. They feel for, and then lock around, a finger or a small rod. Each stimulation results in a lively play with the toes.

smaller, or by moving faster or slower. If you add words, melodies, rhyming verses, or singing to this varied rhythmical play, the child will be drawn into the rhythm of these movements.

Jumping and Striding Exercises

With both hands around the chest, support the child in an upright position so that the toes are just shy of touching the ground. Now move the child up and down so that the toes do touch the ground. The child will actively use the toes in "landing and takeoff." Observe the child's reaction and adjust your stimulation accordingly. The step-like movements of the infant also allow us to recognize the extraordinary gripping action of the toes when the foot touches down. Allow the child to slowly feel forward with a few steps. Practice sessions should always be brief; they should be repeated several times a day. Also use such varied surfaces as soft carpets, fur-like material, grass, and sand.

Exercises Involving Pushing Off the Hands

When holding a child in a vertical position with the head down, the child's arms will reach for the ground. Watch how the hands react when they touch the supportive base. Start your play again. Gently dip the child's body up and down. Hands and fingers will reach for the ground. As early as in the second month of life, a child will display certain motor reflexes after only a few repetitions. A child reacts to this joyful play with happy gurgling and active participation.

Lifting Head in Prone Position and Sliding

Place the child in prone position. With both hands near the spine, gently stroke across the muscles of the back. Again, watch for the child's reaction; the child will lift the head. In this fashion, the child exercises the muscles of the back.

With the palm of your hand, apply light pressure against the sole of the foot; the child counteracts with a push-off motion similar to the way children support themselves in an upright position. Without assistance, the child slides forward on the stomach.

If possible, use a flat, solid mattress for such movement play. The child should be placed in alternating prone and supine positions on a big mattress on the floor as early as in the second month of life. Only while sleeping should a child be protected from exposure to external stimuli and environmental irritants.

4 Refinement of Perception. Watching Moving Objects.

In the first week of life, a child is already attracted to all moving objects. A three-month-old looks with concentration and fascination at moving objects and learns to observe them. Therefore, mobiles are well suited for refining the ability to be attentive and perceptive. These mobiles should not be too small or move too fast. The combined effects of novelty and repetition boost the concentration and the accuracy of observation—a child gradually recognizes the situation at hand. On the other hand, impressions should be changed constantly, for instance, by varying shapes or colors or by changing dynamic effects. The novel effect increases the intensity of object recognition and generates a wealth of experiences.

Each play activity needs a smooth period of familiarization, which includes repetition; the right movement must be chosen for modification and variation. Play with moving objects should never be boring or tiresome. An infant refines sensory perception through impressions of the environment. Placed on a mattress or on a blanket on the floor, the infant will gradually learn to recognize different light effects or moving shapes. The infant learns to stare at objects in order to recognize them.

An especially diversified play object is a ball that is rolled toward the child or moved slowly back and forth before the child's eyes. Noted educator Friedrich Froebel, who founded the concept "kindergarten," labels the ball as the child's "first toy," which helps the child to discover the world through its motion—up and down, back and forth, spinning and rolling away. The child's watchful tracking of the ball's motion displays growing attention. More confident reactions are proof of the child's developing sense of direction.

A moving object always captivates a child's concentration and arouses curiosity. Make sure that the play proceeds quietly and without haste. A child needs time, and the adult needs patience.

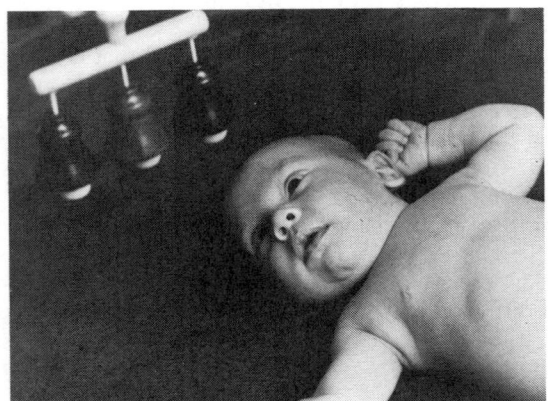

Objects moved in a variety of ways require attention and gradually refine awareness of movement—the object is consciously being recognized and observed.

In the sixth month, children can track a moving object on their own accord; they crawl after a rolling ball and try to grab it. Thus, they learn to propel themselves and to control their own direction at will.

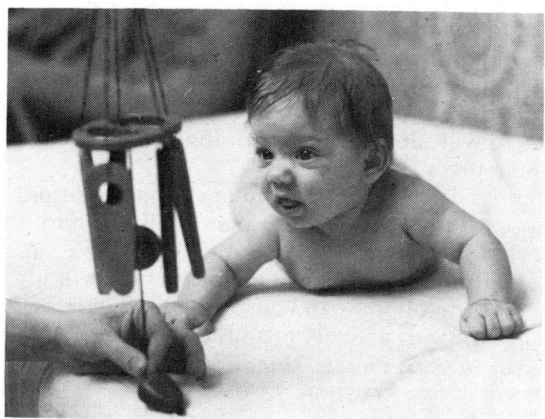

Play objects should not be uniform; they should vary in shape and color. Only then can a child learn to recognize differences.

5 Standing Up Without Help. The Importance of the Crawling Stage. Unsupported Standing as Proof of Balance.

It is all right to help a child in the attempt to stand up, but do not force a child into a sitting or standing position. Children will do this on their own. As they pull themselves up, they may need some assistance in the form of a steady support. We can also offer our fingers or another object for support. The decision to act must come from the child. Patience and cheerful encouragement develop confidence. Do not rush the child and do not offer help beyond what is necessary. Without really comprehending specific words, the child will respond when lovingly addressed. A child will sense praise for trying simply from the inflection in one's voice.

By repeatedly raising their heads from a prone position, along with support from the hands, infants will begin to lift themselves. In the second and third months of life, infants can lift and turn their heads. Gradually, they will lift the upper part of their bodies and raise a hand. The legs and particularly the toes actively push the body forward. From the fourth to sixth month, this sliding will gradually change to a form of free crawling.

Crawling introduces an important new period of orientation in space and the ability not only to change direction, but also to vary one's own speed.

A longer period of crawling, with its many practical experiences in orientation while moving in different directions, promotes eventual, unsupported standing. Parents may introduce variations through innovative crawling games: crawling through a tunnel, through straddled legs, crawling in slalom fashion under tables and chairs, or encounters and evasions.

Children start on their own to crawl up a staircase. Do not hold them back, but be sure you are nearby for protection. Crawling upstairs teaches a child to shift body weight upward. Standing up unsupported is a logical consequence

Unsupported walking, with its shifting from one foot to another, requires a sense of balance. The arms are used for balance, and it is not uncommon for the tongue to "assist" during such concentrated efforts.

of this activity. Thus, crawling upstairs is upright posture training for the seven- to ten-month-old child. An obstacle course with ups and downs—for example, from pillow to a footstool, upward onto a table and then down again across a chair, then to the floor—leads to secure supporting and grasping movements. A child learns through self-discovery and a variety of experiences.

In the crawling stage, the arms are gradually relieved of carrying the load. For example, children may support themselves with one hand only while reaching for a chair with the other. Suddenly, they pull themselves up and stand erect. There is a common rule in this—children have to discover this opportunity on their own and must stand up by themselves. We should provide them with ample opportunities for such attempts.

Higher and higher the child reaches, all the way to the much favored "tippy-toe" position. Now the child has achieved the total stretch.

Standing unsupported for the first time is a precarious test of balance. Children will use their arms for balance when taking their first independent steps. And, as quickly as possible, they will seek out a hold and support. Flanked

A further step toward independence: the shifting of body weight upward and downward. The child learns to walk upstairs and downstairs. The child holds on with just one hand. Soon the child will let go of that support as well.

by two adults, short stepping movements become favorite games. Children need familiar assistants. During these games, the adult should be in a squat position, moving along at eye level with the child. Chairs, tables, and banisters may aid in support.

Left alone, children will develop their own agendas for "walking lessons." Eagerness carries them from one support to another, from bed to chair, from stool to table. Short periods of independent walking are often still alternated with crawling movements. These interludes create the important phases of relief and recovery. Children learn to follow their own rhythm of stress and recovery.

6 Promoting Spontaneity. Further Play With Fingers and Toes. Contact Play.

Self-reliance means promoting spontaneity in the child, the inner driving force of a child. The readiness of children to act independently, to try without urging, is awakened through interesting situations. Children practice and collect learning experiences. At the same time, movements, sounds, and noises can be experienced simultaneously, such as a ball that jingles while being rolled, a doll that squeaks when pressed, or a rattle that makes noises when shaken.

Children often play spontaneously with their fingers and toes. They touch and test, and learn about themselves through "body play." Children will grab one of their toes and suck on it, and often use tongue and mouth as instruments of discovery. Small children often continue to move their tongues when faced with difficult situations.

All games are amplified through repetition and through changes in movement impulses, which in turn lead to new types of play. The result is play that continues "indefinitely," that is, play that allows for constant variations of the fundamental elements. Practice situations can lead spontaneously to play, as long as performance and demand levels are not perceived as unattainable or, conversely, too easily attained, thus losing their attraction.

All play can involve contact if the child's play partner can adapt to it, for example, in hide and seek, the disappearing, the search and discovery. Children also instinctively comprehend the "funny part" of a game. In turn, a joyous feeling about the mere idea of the game and its humorous aspects forms the foundation for creativity in the play-learn process.

Movement games in the first months and years of life—and indeed all enticements for play—are based upon imagination. They should not proceed "monotonously"; rather, they should be carefully executed. Any change in space, rhythm, time, and force stimulates reactions that children have not previously experienced.

These refined and expanded movements, achieved through different challenges and their corresponding reactions, later determine the quality of the movement performance. The skill and fast reaction ability of children in later behavior depend on their earlier experiences and perceptions.

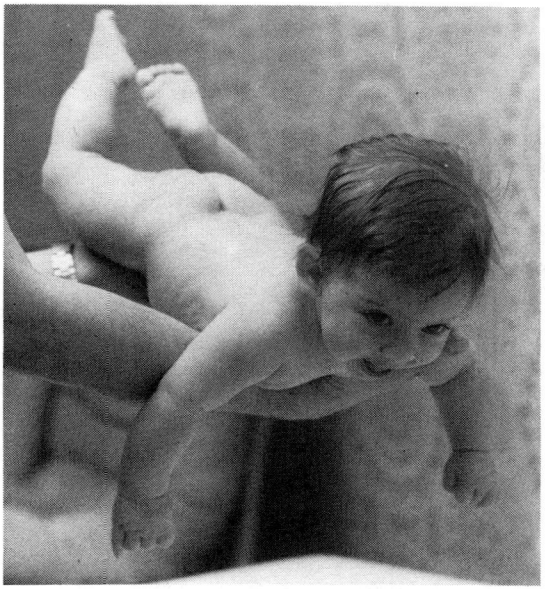

The adult is the play partner, motivating the child to try new experiences; for example, crawling downward from a chair or bed to the floor head first, body weight securely cushioned with both hands.

Following are examples of contact play in the first year of life (partners observe the children's reactions):
- Partners let the children hang from their hands and gently swing them between their legs or from side to side in front of their bodies.
- Partners let the children climb up their bodies, step by step across thighs, stomach, and chest.
- Partners allow the children to experience up and down rhythmical movements while riding upon their laps, intensifying or decreasing the impulses.
- Children are held in head-down positions, and then are raised and lowered to a point where they are helping support their own weight.

The impulses emanating from the adult partner should

The partner assists the child to spring from bed onto floor and changes the rhythm and dynamics of the movement: faster or slower, stronger in takeoff, or smoother and softer. What is important are children's reactions, feelings, and joy.

always be in tune with the desires and reactions of the child. The partner should always wait with patience and sensitivity for the spontaneous reaction of the child. This way, the child will intentionally grasp a situation and its attendant movement, thereby guiding the fun of the game. A person actively participating will be associated with the joy of the game. The child is happy if father or mother is ready for another game. The child vigorously expresses eagerness for additional play and sometimes even anger if the game is ended too soon.

7 Coordination: Testing Balance, Responses. Variations of Accomplished Motor Skills. Orientation in Space.

The importance of coordination in the development of the child cannot be emphasized enough. Therefore, the concept is explained once more in detail. It contains three components:
• sense of balance;
• ability to react;
• adjustment to a given situation.

Coordination means one is skillful and able to react quickly and appropriately at the right moment. The lack of independence in a child's everyday behavior is always based on missed learning opportunities. Due to an educator's misconstrued protectiveness and the lack of understanding of a child's needs, the wonderful movement capabilities of children in the early learning stages often remain underdeveloped. Since adults often approach specific tasks with inhibition and restrictions relative to psychomotor experiences, they also prevent the child from independently mastering tempting ventures.

This applies especially to balancing experiments. Small children exploit all opportunities to "be off balance"—they tumble, fall, and learn to get back up without help until they again stand in a balanced position. Rushing in to help means calling a halt to these essential experiences. Avoid unnecessary assistance, but remain attentive and watchful of children to instill in them a feeling of nearness and security.

A moving base of support helps children to become more sensitive to finding their balance: they bounce on a mattress, purposely dropping down and rebounding, or tumble from a step onto a pillow. This rebounding play is repeated over and over again until the "fun" sinks in. After that, children need new games with increasing degrees of difficulty.

In particular, meaningful ball games help children acquire fast reactions. They track the direction of the ball—

where and how it rolls and how fast it moves—and react quickly or slowly, confidently or insecurely. They learn to judge unfamiliar movements and to adjust their own movement accordingly.

The child's skills are promoted through a variety of movement patterns such as changing from walking to crawling and through orientation in space such as upward or downward or moving around in a circle without losing the sense of direction.

Variations of already acquired movement skills are important for the development of improved coordination. For instance, children need balls made of different materials and sizes. Balls made of cloth, rubber, paper, and leather require different reactions to their respective movement patterns. The various movement impulses applied by children increasingly refine their control and accuracy. As a result, children will become more self-assured and able to play in new and unfamiliar situations.

Orientation in space initially occurs subconsciously. Gradually, this orientation in space, in conjunction with acquired movement skills, leads to open space awareness and can be incorporated in play. For instance, a hill is more interesting than a level surface because of the many potential movement combinations it offers—climbing uphill, running and rolling downhill, tumbling and turning. These combinations of up, down, and around can be expanded from open-ended play to self-contained play that involves rules.

Children should also experience and learn about the limits of their ability. Adventures should be precarious, but in a way that they can be mastered. Those who "build

The first tests of balance require support, especially when the child ventures onto difficult territory such as a narrow brick wall, a teetering plank, or a bouncy mattress.

fences around children"—for the sake of safety—will hamper their future behavior. Children need to experience independence so that they can master difficult situations. They must also learn to overcome negative experiences, misfortune, or clumsiness. When children fall down, then rise and repeat a previously unsuccessful attempt—minus the self-pity—they will learn to recognize their own potential; they know what they are capable of and how to overcome their own incompetence.

8 Suppression of Movement Exploration Creates Handicaps. The Importance of Climbing Experiences and Gripping Efficiency. Gaining Strength Through Hanging and Swinging.

All newly acquired movement skills simultaneously represent an emotional and cognitive learning experience: children experience self-assurance, joy, and happiness and gain new knowledge; they learn to overcome obstacles as well as to take action when playing with partners and to independently find their own way around. These experiences move them steadily toward independence—"I can let go, I can do it myself. . . ." This is a natural reaction in children when trying to master a new task on their own. Experiencing success or failure is learning through self-discovery. Preventing experimentation in the early learning stages leads to inhibited behavior. Examples of this are climbing experiences; while climbing, children move to a higher level, looking at a new world. They feel exalted; they tower above the adult. Children around the age of two have a great desire to climb. Likewise, in high performance sports a different climbing route is worth the effort; one voluntarily seeks danger and selects complicated and risky ascents even though there are simpler ways to reach the summit.

Equipment meant for climbing is often incorrectly constructed. It should be neither too rigid nor too low. An elastic base of support and random, rather than standard, ways of climbing up and down provide stimulation and make it possible to vary the movement pattern. Good climbing skills will only develop where new combinations stimulate the child's world of discovery and movement abilities.

Swiss architect Kurt Braegger designed ideal climbing

Climbing means movement efficiency. In order to practice safe gripping and supporting, a chair or sofa is used initially to shift the body weight.

trees for the apes of the Basel Zoo. The elastic branches of these trees can carry loads of more than 200 pounds; yet, through their elasticity, they provide the necessary rebound. Playgrounds should be equipped with similar equipment. Often, standardized play equipment at public playgrounds contradicts all rules of play pedagogy, rules that promote self-reliant exploration and creativity.

Children like pliable ropes, rope ladders, and swings because they can easily master them. Sureness of grip and the strength to hold on are developed without instructions. Children will repeat their attempts and trials on their own if encouraged by other children or when they learn to set things in motion on their own.

Of course, children need safety precautions; they must learn how to behave in dangerous situations. However, children should not be stopped pointlessly through admonitions or threats such as "watch out, you will fall" or "you better stay down here, you will break a leg!"

Outside help should only be offered if required as a necessary impetus to master the task. It is more important for children to try unsuccessfully to climb onto a swing 10 to 20 times before they suddenly succeed rather than to end this problem-solving effort through a success they have not achieved on their own.

Children develop their support and hanging ability through climbing, hanging, and swinging. Torsal strength assures upright posture and prevents postural weakness. *Children who climb do not have postural weakness.* They are able to handle their body weight.

Carrying, pulling, and pushing can also be suggested and systematically supported as activities to strengthen the torso:

Climbing nets are suitable climbing apparatus for two- and three-year-olds. They are not rigid and therefore require refined responses. Each shift in equilibrium improves awareness of movement and thus confidence.

Inhibited movement experiences create handicaps. Climbing during the early childhood period is important for self-confidence, for the ability to accurately assess a situation, and for an increased feeling of success. Extended experience in climbing is achieved only through diversified play involving all sorts of climbing situations.

- lifting an object and carrying it from one location to another;
- carrying something on the head or the back;
- pulling each other across a line or into a circle during play;
- pulling one's own body weight forward and upward on a smooth bench;
- pushing away an adult; this play should be enforced by the bigger and stronger partner because the changing stimuli of force results in more assured movement impulses.

9 Learning Movement Patterns Through Active Participation and Imitation. Movement Perception.

How do children learn to move skillfully? Just like other beginners, they must develop a sense of conscious imagination. Starting with instinctive participation and imitation, a clearly defined movement image is gradually developed through observation.

Participation, accomplished, for example, by being carried, represents an initial introductory phase of the movement process. Adaptation or self-adjustment to an unfamiliar movement pattern is also used in later phases of learning through movement, as when a helper guides the hand of the learner, or an adult protectively hugs a child close during a downhill ski run, or a child is given support during sledding by leaning against the person guiding the sled.

Imitation of movements is not just confined to early childhood alone. Movement patterns are experienced not just through active participation, but also through observation. The impetus for the learner's own practical exploration comes either through a role model or with the aid of pictures, movies, and conscious perception of technical problems or tricks. The proportion of learning through active participation or learning through observation is about 50/50. With respect to infants, the percentage of learning through imitation is probably more extensive.

Three-year-olds are fascinated when they can watch novel activities: for instance, curbside rubbish removal, the sweeping of streets, the laying of tiles on floors. Children enjoy taking part in polishing shoes, cleaning up, and setting the table. To do the same work as an adult strengthens children's self-confidence, especially when they take on this work voluntarily. For many children, helping adults in their work can double as play as well as substitute for other play action needs. What is important here is the type of activity. Modern, activity-oriented playgrounds also aim at offering children responsibilities in such areas as caring for animals, including cleaning of stables, feeding, and grooming, or skilled workmanship and handicraft applied in the construction of play houses or play furniture.

Why do children always enjoy lifting and carrying something or dragging a load? They try to overcome obstacles. They push and pull heavy objects and test the limits of their potential.

Critical observation alone will gradually lead to clear and conscious movement perception. Especially helpful are probing questions that further clarify the proceedings: "Did you watch how Peter took off?" "Why did Karen use both hands?" "Is it easier to hit the target with the small or the big ball?"

Children who jointly participate in sports with their parents, or accompany them often to sporting events, very clearly perceive special actions as well as techniques, for example, the shooting of goals in soccer or such special tactics as offense, defense, and drills. They also learn to describe the process verbally, often more clearly than their teacher. Therefore, it is rather sad when educators of children in their early learning years personally have no clear conceptions of the movement processes and are unable to illustrate them through appropriate examples or through pointed questions.

Toddlers learn through imitation and show surprising movement skills. Through observation and comparisons, they instinctively use the appropriate techniques. They kick the soccer ball; they take a sharp turn with the scooter or the bicycle; and they slalom skillfully on their skis.

Here are some examples of learning by observation:
- Children observe each other—by chance on the playground or purposefully in the classroom.
- Children observe pictures found in books or on posters. Sports texts with their related picture stories illustrate particular movement skills and clearly stress the focal points of the various learning stages. Instructions can be read aloud or worked out by the children as soon as they are able to read on their own.
- Children observe sporting events and movement action on television. This immediately confronts them with questions that further hold their attention.
- Children observe themselves in a mirror and learn to recognize themselves from a distance. This type of learning, if properly stimulated, can also contribute to understanding one's own movement performance.
- Children mirror each other, copying exactly the movements of other children. The intention in this case is to use one's observational ability to practice quick adaptability.

10 Perceptual Learning. Numerous Variations in Perception. Activity With Balloons. Examples for the Distinction of Direction, Shape, Speed, and Space.

Observation and imitation are not the only means to improve perceptual learning. Perception can be achieved through:
• visual means, i.e., sight;
• auditory means, i.e., hearing;
• tactile means, i.e., touch;
and through many combinations of the above.

In the earliest months of childhood, tactile stimulation, that is, the touching, handling, and holding of the child, predominates. Through this stimulation, the child learns sensory perception and to distinguish between various perceptions, for example, that one hand is more rugged than another and grips more firmly; that one person is rougher and the other more sensitive in his or her approach. The words, rhythms, or sounds that accompany specific movements will strengthen the senses and render them more sensitive.

The objective of learning through observation, also known as perceptual learning, is to refine the conception of movement. A rich variety of impressions should be presented whenever possible; variations of speed combined with different changes in direction and variable dynamics lead to a variety of new movements. An illustrative example is activity with balloons, which demonstrates different ways of propulsion through use of hands, fingers, feet, and knees, as well as different movement impulses through throwing, striking, finger snapping, and rebounding. Yet another example involves different ways of swinging, for instance, while sitting, standing, as part of a seesawing twosome, or inside an automobile tire. Invent all sorts of games with variable perception to expand the child's ability to learn.

Here one sees two children swinging rhythmically in unison on a movable apparatus in a very unsafe way. Yet, the risk represents stimulation, arousing an interest in mastering the situation.

With concentrated effort, the child begins a slide "into the unknown." Desire and fear are equally balanced, but fun and curiosity win out.

Also necessary are stimuli that intentionally force the child to make distinctions, to compare and to evaluate. Is it easier to jump on the floor, on a mat, or on a trampoline? The next step in learning is to question "why?" In order to achieve the highest degree of recall possible with respect to these differentiations, we often ask children, upon conclusion of their activities, to interpret different situations through use of descriptions, modeling, or drawing. Accuracy is not really as important as the realization that there are differences. In time, these are recognized with assurance. This perception conveys a clear message of what is happening or what is planned. Linked to this should be an acquired perception. Does the action one takes concur with that which one planned to do? Three-year-olds are often more critical of themselves or others than are adults, as, for example, when they ride their scooters around obstacles, or when they try to shoot for a certain area with a ball, or during the well-known game of hopscotch.

Three-year-olds should be able to distinguish between the following:
- movement direction: forward, backward, sideways, and around;
- form of movement (pathways): moving in a circle, in a curve (semi-circle), zig-zag running, forming an alley, running through an arch;
- change of speed: slow, fast, hurried, haltingly, gliding;
- orientation in space: up, down, in front, behind, left and right, low and high, narrow and wide, square, round.

Balloons help to refine the ability to direct and to control because their slow flight enables the child to clearly observe and control them. Versatile tasks entice children to come up with their own ideas. Any part of the body can be used as an instrument of play.

Through these perceptions children discover new psychomotor actions and activities that they combine on their own:
- climbing quickly onto a high table and climbing down slowly;
- hitting a triangular target on a wall with a ball, and then a square-shaped target;
- carrying glasses filled with water through an obstacle course, followed by a change in the course;
- balancing a tennis ball on a spoon while climbing a ladder and placing it in a container;
- playing hopscotch on surfaces marked with painted shapes.

11 Sufficient Time for Play. Ability to Play Implies Concentration. Invitation to Play Is More Important Than Directed Play.

Children learn to play only if offered enough time to devote to the action of play. Only when a child knows how to manipulate play objects will they lend themselves to use in play. Natural stimuli for play are curiosity, encounter with the unknown, imaginative rearrangement of mastered skills, fun, and creative joy. New knowledge is always gained through experiencing an event and through control of a situation.

As they run back and forth and up and down a hill, children create their own games to entertain themselves or involve others. Each motor pattern develops into a game if it can be repeated over and over again and can be altered at will by the child. Tumbling around on the ground or a combination of "climbing up a step and jumping down" turns into a game as a result of repeated movement and through the transformation of movement characteristics invented by the child through innovative play. Play involves freedom as well as limitations. To be able to act freely is a prerequisite for all play even at the rudimentary level, and the repeatability of a game results only from its limitations.

Infants play with their fingers as soon as they recognize finger play as their very own and are able to direct it.
Play becomes a game only through rules. Traditional rules of a game originally developed from spontaneous, self-invented rules. Eventually these rules permit larger group participation.

The ability to play means devotion to a procedure and consequently also means concentration. This explains why children often appear rather serious and sensible when following the objectives of a game or while creating a certain game situation. They become engrossed in the process and try to familiarize themselves with its characteristics through repeated trials and experiments. They learn to

The combination of climbing and carrying is being mastered surefootedly by these three- and four-year-olds. During this task they display an intense level of concentration.

"handle" play objects, for instance, a new ball, a hoop, a kite, a bell, and then begin to use them.

Experimenting with unfamiliar apparatus is important. During experimentation, children demonstrate highly

Horizontal bars are favorite play apparatus of five- and six-year-olds. Their ideas are surprising. They invent new forms of hip pullovers, backward hip circles, and forward and backward single knee swings. Like bats, children are comfortable hanging upside down.

developed skills which no adult could possibly have demonstrated to them. The same applies to prolonged experimentation on high bars by six- and seven-year-olds or to an artistic performance with hoops or ropes. Each of these activities requires continuous concentration during the learning process. Play initiatives result in ever increasing learning impulses because the progress achieved is so obvious. Self-approval based on one's own ability and on learning from each other by observing originates in the "social domain," in partnerships and in groups. From the age of three on, the child needs play initiative within a play association.

The challenge to play is more important than directed play. Through independent probing and through trial and error, the child will achieve self-realization. The ideas of children often surprise us. For example, children invent:
• rolling on their stomachs on top of balls;
• one-legged knee hangs on the horizontal bar;
• different games using cans to practice balancing.

Rolling barrels, cans, or wastebaskets offers challenges for balancing. Playing skills are refined through differentiated choice of play equipment.

12. Sound and Movement. Monotonous Activities as Stepping Stones to Rhythmics. Development of an Individualized Expression of Sound.

Sound and movement are closely linked to each other. Initially, the child produces little more than babbling, a monotony of syllables. Gradually, autonomous rhythmics are developed that are audible and visible through their association with accentuated movements. Rhythmic monotony is an ancient tool for accentuating movement processes, a kind of stimulus to intensify or to diminish a movement process, thereby controlling the movement. It is movement control, not in a sense of perfectly timed technique, but rather one of freely improvised movement dynamics.

Infants, too, often display loud sound impulses as they kick their arms and legs, cooing and gurgling to express their joy, or conversely to express resentment and anger.

Children take advantage of every opportunity to make sounds. Many of these possibilities are discovered purely by accident, for instance by:
- tapping together wooden blocks or sticks;
- playfully hitting a pot with a cooking spoon;
- setting wind chimes into motion.

The monotony of these repetitive actions is often nerve wracking to adults, but for children this monotonous type of play is an important step toward self-sustained rhythmical patterning of their movements.

The child's involvement is determined by the rhythm of the music. In countries with lively folklore, for instance, in South America, Mexico, and Africa, three-year-olds are not shy about dancing rhythmically along within the immediate family circle. In families that make music together, the hearing of the child unconsciously becomes so keen that by the age of three, the child can easily master musical scales and melodies. According to more recent findings, musical talent is the result of earlier experiences.

Knocking and hammering with the use of an object lead to coordination of sound and movement. Children learn to combine the force of their pounding with the dynamics of the generated sounds. This results in the creation of original rhythms.

Infants growing up with lots of music develop hearing abilities different from those who rarely hear musical melodies. The same applies to tone; screaming children are the result of having to listen to screaming and to undifferentiated projected sound.

The teaching of children's songs often prevents children from using their own initiative to develop their own style of sound. Like range of movement, which is initially limited but is followed by expansion from month to month, the child's range of sound and tone is at first limited to a few elements, such as, for example, the five note scale. Despite these limited abilities, children are learning to play as demonstrated by the following examples: question and answer games in the form of a movement game; a rhythmical or musical game; and teasing games accompanied by high- and low-pitched tones. Later, movements

A humming top elicits surprise and curiosity. In time, children will recognize the connection between their actions and the spinning of the top.

Because of their differentiated sounds, humming, chirping, and rustling noises are especially fascinating to a child.

It seems easier to carry a load when accompanied by loud "ahs and ohs." Similarly, weight lifters shout loudly to boost their strength.

are continuously accompanied by rhythmically accentuated sounds:
- running softly, running softly . . .
- stomping loudly, stomping loudly . . .
- stepping tip-tap, tip-tap . . .
- up and down and up and down and . . .
- hop, hop, gallop, gallop, hop, hop . . .

Children are supposed to find their own rhythms; some imitate adults and eventually come up with their own "rhyme."

13 Examples for Situational Learning Exeriences. The "Infant Jumper," Sled Riding, and Swinging. The Learning of Complex Actions.

Thus far, we have briefly covered adaptive learning through moving along and moving alone—learning through imitation, observation, and perception as tools for differentiation of perceptive abilities and movement control. Now let me describe an additional concept, namely: *situational learning*. This type of learning does not deal with separate accomplishments, but rather behavior within a given situation. It requires that basic movement experiences are applied at the right moment and are appropriate to a given situation.

Within the last few years, the "infant jumper" has become one of the simplest play stimulants for six- to eight-month-old infants. With this jumper, infants, aided by their push-off ability, learn to direct their own movement in a limited way. The jumper intensifies their push-off in such a way that they can move themselves in different directions. They use their flexible toes for propulsion. The toe muscles, especially the ones which bend and splay, are in control of erect postural carriage. Infants who move around a lot in "jumper" fashion gain preliminary skills that later will facilitate their orientation in space while jumping on a springy mattress or on a trampoline.

This transference from one acquired technique to another is successful only if the movement elements are similar, as for example, during the transition from scooter riding to riding a bicycle or from roller skating to ice skating, or from trampolining to diving.

Children who climb a hill with their sleds and then, at the right moment, want to sit or lie on them, need a wealth of different situational experiences; they need to learn how to change a given situation, for instance, by changing the riding position or by braking or increasing the speed. The more creative children are in making these changes, the greater the refinement of movement sense

Sled riding provides constantly changing situations depending upon whether the hill is steep or flat, uneven or smooth, and on the condition of the snow. In addition, there is the effect of the child's own action during push-off and reinforcement of the momentum through leaning forward or backward. Here again, children stick out their tongues to "help" in concentrating on this task.

and movement intelligence. Another example is found in different forms of swinging: first on the hands of an adult partner or on the knees of an adult; eventually this swinging turns into swinging on one's own, with increasing impulses, with counter movements, and into play with a partner or a group. The elementary swinging motion grows into complex situations with a wider and wider range. The goal is independent utilization of learned accomplishments in complex actions.

Each learning situation should change periodically and should be expanded and offered with more challenging and interesting tasks. If children have enough time and space for playing, they will often come up with these possibilities on their own.

Complex actions will be mastered through situational learning and without conscious analysis of particular combinations. Like a soccer player who together with others first learns easy combinations of offensive and defensive play in front of the goal, the child is in need of situational

At the age of six months the child in the "infant jumper" is able to move independently; the child changes the direction and pushes off strongly and purposefully with the feet. Training in the "infant jumper" promotes jumping ability.

experiences from which techniques and action strategies can be developed. These are eventually recalled and used for critical corrections.

The situational learning experience illustrates the combinations of several movement patterns that require versatile change of speed, with space and direction components, as well as flexible, differentiated control. Spontaneous necessary reactions are first learned through situations—for example, by dodging at the right moment, by picking up a rolling ball without stopping, by following a rolling hoop and crawling through it without touching it, or by driving narrow slalom curves with a scooter or a bicycle while meeting and dodging other drivers.

The situational learning experience is enhanced through the social aspects of consideration and support from partners or groups. The actions must be in tune and in harmony with those of others. Through movement play, a child learns to get along with others and to respect the initiative and reactions of other players.

14 Sports Activities Requiring Balance: Riding a Scooter, Roller Skating, Bicycling, Ice Skating, and Snow Skiing.

In Chapter 7 we examined the development of coordination, the neuromuscular control system that affects balance, reaction ability, and situational adaptation. Let us now specifically emphasize those sports activities and types of movement that require balance and therefore promote the child's sense of motor equilibrium to the greatest extent.

The following sports belong to the group which requires balancing skills: riding a scooter, roller skating, bicycling, ice skating, snow skiing, and swimming. The very first independent step is one of the most difficult tests of balance—the child has to stand up, remain standing, and be able to transfer weight from one foot to another. Two-year-olds look for new challenges; they move their base of support by using a scooter. Using basic skills they achieve new levels of learning. The tasks are systematically intensified by:
- rolling downhill while changing the speed or with sudden change of direction;
- riding a scooter around obstacles in slalom fashion;
- meeting and dodging.

Three- and four-year-olds learn to use tricycles or bicycles with little difficulty, especially if there is evidence that they have mastered the task of proper balance on a scooter. Active control of speed through one's own push-off movement leads to new understanding—children learn to control the applied speed and to safely steer their vehicles. Actually, children should prepare themselves for road traffic through
- pulling up and stopping;
- avoiding obstacles and changing direction.

During roller and ice skating, the difficulties are much greater. The footing is unstable, the feet slide and roll and glide away from underneath the body. Children learn to adjust their bodies into a gliding and rolling motion so that their upright body position and balance are maintained. Roller and ice skating require specially prepared play surfaces, usually asphalt, or ice, to fully utilize the gliding effect. Skaters must be able to perpetuate rather than retard their gliding motion by using their own momentum. As in pedaling a scooter or a bicycle, roller and ice skating necessitate movement with long striding legwork and a strong take-off from the foot as well as unsupported body position and extended arms.

Gliding movements on ice have a special stimulating character, which is the reason why children love to "flit" across the ice. They use a very intense and fast take-off to set their body weight in motion. Children are born speed skaters. They learn to change direction; movement is directed forward and backward in a variety of ways and is then connected through curves, loops, and with jumps.

Thus, it is recommended to choose and emphasize scooters and tricycles for two- and three-year-olds and roller and ice skating for five- and six-year-olds to act in promoting balance proficiency.

Bicycling, ice skating, and snow skiing have become national and family sports. Parents become partners and their capabilities are often surpassed by their five- and six-year-old children. This, too, is an important learning experience that reinforces the self-assurance of the child. Chapter 20 deals in greater detail with the possibilities of family play.

While ice skating, children instinctively experience adults' gliding rhythm and try to move along rhythmically. Children need partners for movement games—they learn through observation, imitation, and participation.

15 Learning Through Problem Solving. Positive and Negative Aggressive Behavior. Self-Awareness Leading to Self-Confidence.

Conflicts are a part of mastering life. In a child's life, conflicts should be neither avoided nor withheld; a child must learn to overcome conflicts. Can I? Should I? Will I do? Children instinctively ask themselves these questions when facing unknown situations such as jumping into a swimming pool, climbing over a fence, climbing atop a wall, first trials on the trampoline. All these are movement problems that have to be solved.

Recognizing that there are several solutions and being uncertain about how to solve a problem provides new challenges. Understanding this "problem solving" method is a learning technique in teaching sports. Depending upon the level of performance, this can take place either on the most elementary or on the most advanced level. Solving "open-ended problems," which may have several solutions, and overcoming one's own conflicts, will result in autonomous behavior, which children must acquire on their own. This process is expressed by the word "emancipation." Gaining self-assurance and recognizing and fulfilling one's own responsibility are goals that can only be achieved through the problem-solving approach. Regimented education and noncritical adoption of behavioral standards, just because they are decreed and enforced, will hamper the development of intelligence.

Aggression and aggressiveness are a part of this emancipation because self-awareness will not be accomplished without the desire to overcome existing resistance. The fun of arguing, rivalry, and the quest for achievement can mean mental power for a child. Rivalry is a form of communication and of interpersonal relationship that strives to achieve one's own perfection through comparative measures. Yet, the child does not think about real comparisons expressed in terms of measurements and numbers. Running with the intent to come in first, jump-

Jumping down gives the child a happy feeling similar to that of an adult who flies. Again and again, children look for slopes or climbing apparatus with greater height from which they can jump.

ing, climbing, romping, and lust for fighting are all forms of self-challenge and are based on a natural willingness to put oneself to the test.

Aggressiveness expressed as a desire to hurt, to insult, and to put down others is the result of inferior education. A child who tries to harm others again and again has no self-confidence and tries to "show off" artificially and violently. Contests and competitions therefore offer a possibility to control one's own behavior. A group at play that is interfered with will expel a troublemaker; "We don't like to play with you anymore." The self-destructive aggressive child definitely needs more self-confidence.

Self-awareness leads to self-confidence and consequently to recognition of one's own mistakes and weaknesses. Weakness, once recognized, fosters the urge for self-conquest; "Next time I will do it better . . ." "My fingers are still so clumsy. . . ." Skiing children or judo groups are good examples; one can easily detect the incentives for learning—one's own clumsiness is readily acknowledged because others have their own weaknesses, too.

Children are often misled by misunderstood protectiveness. Children are told "you are doing an excellent job" when they should actually be told "it will take just a little longer, but soon you will do it." Pseudo-childlike treatment often results in striking the wrong note through down playing or glorification; by doing this, children fail to learn how to quickly size up the real situation. Children who later face a critical assessment of actions for which they had always previously been praised will be subjected to a conflict, which is difficult to overcome. The results are rejection, anger, and frustration. They rush back to the person who did all the praising and complain about the new person who is more critically inclined.

16 Imaginary and Creative Movement Ideas. Learning Through Discovery.

All sports and play activities, as well as all forms of dance, were created as a result of human imagination. In sports, imaginary anticipation determines the action. In ball games, for instance, the thrower must aim the ball at the spot where the thrower thinks the catcher will be able to catch it at the right time. Or, the defensive player must recognize where the ball is going by the way the offensive player releases the ball. The same principle applies also to the running long jump, bicycling, and games with balloons.

Movement ideas always originate from the joyful feeling about one's creative abilities, about tricks, and unique variations. Newer forms of sports, for example, trampolining, ski flying, or scuba diving, were created as a result of our desire to achieve something that had never been accomplished before. This applies equally, although with other standards, to children's play. Anyone who would round up the abundance of ideas produced as a result of children's creativity would end up with an admirable movement methodology and an astounding collection of games.

To use an example, children use a simple barrel for balancing as well as for rolling forward while sitting inside. Empty cans are so combined in their set up that they become stepping stones for practicing balance. With the help of a rope strung back and forth several times, an elastic bridge emerges, which can be crossed.

Children develop imaginary movement only through repeated and unhampered trials. Nothing will inhibit imagination more than passed on traditional games, in particular the customary circle games and song plays. These games hardly offer any freedom for improvisation and self-creation. On the other hand, providing a number of balls in different sizes can lead to new ideas for games. Also, a combination of planks, barrels, and old automobile tires can be utilized as seesaws and cat walks, creating new movement situations, which combine skills and imagination into an idea for a new game.

How does the world look from an upside-down position? Headstand variations are already done at an early age, demonstrating learning by discovery.

Six-year-olds master hula hoop play with artistic skill. They smoothly direct the swinging hoop forward or backward without stopping the motion.

"Learning by discovery" offers vital assistance for teaching and learning to play. Children should be allowed to discover and should be given the opportunity and freedom to handle materials, objects, and equipment on their own. Some play objects are rather exclusively programmed and do not allow independent and imaginative action. A typical example on playgrounds is the so-called Viking swing on which the children just sit and are moved in unison. This contrasts with a merry-go-round, which must be pushed by a few with the others sitting. The "Giant Stride" gym swing provides much more stimulating opportunities because one can push off forcefully without help from others and be carried to any height desired.

Rotation possibilities using a ring are discovered by a five-year-old "artist." At the same time, the child moves hand and foot.

Movement ideas and movement imagination are often stifled by safety precautions, and misconstrued attention takes away the child's freedom of play. A certain willingness to take risks has to stimulate play on playgrounds. Right from the start, a child's imagination must not be hampered by prohibitory signs, such as "Ball Playing Not Allowed."

What is the best way to skillfully move the barrel with one's feet so that it rolls forward, stops, and also rolls backward?

17 Play Activities and Play Concepts. Cooperation in Group Play.

Chapters 11 and 13 explained how individual skills gradually develop into more complex actions. There is no game without action and no action without the concept of the game. Running and ball games are the most favored play activities at the preschool age. They offer an abundance of possible variations and the appeal of an original game idea is provided through modified equipment or a changed environment. Running games involve such activities as fleeing, catching up, tagging, returning, hiding, seeking, and finding as play ideas with modified actions. Toddlers, too, are included in the games of older children, as well as adults as playing partner of the child.

Some of the more competitive games have been modified into "mini-games" for eight- to twelve-year-olds. The example set by the older ones as well as performances seen on television or on playgrounds lead children to methodological cognitive playing. Five- and six-year-olds, together with parents or in groups of partners, practice their soccer games in specific simplified action units, such as:
• offense and defense near the goal;
• passing the ball and dribbling;
• trapping and kicking the ball.

Basketball, tennis, and hockey have also turned into games played by children. Simplified equipment that encourages play, such as a basket attached high on a garage or on a wall, lead to practice while "passing by." A stone, a ball, or a tin can are propelled forward with plain sticks that are also used to mark a goal. Children in China play table tennis as early as the kindergarten age. A door lifted from its frame becomes the table and a few bricks placed in an upright position replace the net. This creates partnerships and improves playing skills without an instructor. It is a consequence of a traditional play culture that is cultivated in different countries in different ways, similar to how the song and dance culture is accepted by a family's small child. The child then copies it, discovers that it is possible, and accepts it. Even the sport of tennis, which was formerly reserved for adults only, intrudes more and

Large economy-size cans from a cafeteria serve as multipurpose play equipment for slalom and obstacle course running and jumping.

Stacked on top of each other they serve as targets for target practice games.

more into the world of play for eight-year-olds. Indeed, sports are one of the best initiators of family play policies.

Learning how to act while playing within a group is only possible when the individual child feels capable of interacting with others. Children have to adjust their own strength and agility to those of others and recognize game objectives within the total action, as well as perceive the mutual effort that is required. It makes a difference whether a group of children is asked to cooperate without knowledge of a recognizable goal or whether the group understands the interrelationships within a game complex that children can comprehend on their own and whose meaning they understand. Herein lies the difference. Different types of games result from meaningful activities that a child experiences in daily life, such as the pulling game, a confrontation of strength exemplified by pulling away from a partner using a small rope or hoop, or involving a tug of war with larger groups. The "struggle over a

Flour sacks used for sack races are as interesting a material for group play as are sheets of newspaper that flutter during running. In both activities, speed needs to be coordinated.

medicine ball" or pulling someone inside of a circle or onto a "magic" island are actually elements for variations of the same game category—"who is the strongest?" Other game variations are those involving hoops that roll or fly through the air combined with activities such as running through or around the rolling hoop or a skillful jump into the center of a rolling hoop.

A special passion for playing a certain game often originates from watching tricks performed by one or two children who motivate others to try them too. A typical example is the hula hoop craze, which grabbed hold of children and adults all over the world. Even today, children are still ingeniously trying to keep the hoop's rotations going around their taut bodies; only adults have given up this game.

18 Playing Together, Action and Interaction. Children Look for Companionship During Play. Partnership and Cooperation.

Previous chapters frequently addressed *team play* and actions with assigned roles, as well as children's understanding of their own behavior. This is also known as action and interaction, clearly indicating how one's own activity is linked with that of one or several others in a unit.

Such interactions already begin with the infant through contact with an adult and in movement actions and reactions. Therefore, the first interactions with children and the manner in which they are treated are decisive factors in the development of a child's instinctive attitude toward a partner. Anxiety and timidity are acquired through education and are emotionally transmitted. The same applies to the positive personality traits of spontaneity, independence, joy in play, risk, and awareness of one's abilities.

Addressing the child, followed by conversation, discussion, or even dispute, provides indispensable encouragement for the development of language skills and a differentiated style of self-expression. This applies equally to the quality of movement—either being moved or as one's own activity in joint action with others. Playing next to each other develops into play with each other, which also includes playing against each other.

Children look for the companionship of others, as well as of adults. Children should never be teamed in a one-sided manner, for example, by only playing with their mothers or with children of the same age. The ability to communicate, the willingness to open up to others through play action and to include others in their own play, has to be developed systematically. Many children won't let go of their mother's hands, for instance, when entering nursery school or when meeting an unfamiliar group. A child who has been prepared through partnership and communica-

Two children carry a third child—how can this task best be tackled?

tion curiously searches for new situations, even if they are unfamiliar. The child will first observe from a distance, but will also be without fear.

An only child often lacks the natural, daily experiences of interaction with others. On the other hand, large families with several adults and children offer a chance to experience a variety of communicative opportunities, which in turn provide a wealth of contacts, especially in the first months and years of life. This "open," uninhibited preparation later helps the child to acquire a cosmopolitan attitude.

The adult has to learn to respect the child as a "partner," as somebody to be asked such questions as "Can you?" "Would you like to?" Mutual consideration is essen-

Mutual assistance presents a difficult problem for five-year-olds. This kind of cooperation must be learned systematically.

Passing balloons to a partner through a hoop requires a carefully measured return tap.

tial because contacts must also include "tact" in the sense of mutual respect. Unfortunately, in the relationship between adults and children, the old proverb "it is the tone that makes the music" is sometimes also observed in the negative sense, as, for example, when one nervously yells "you will get it," or when the child has just been scolded with "you are too clumsy." It would be more appropriate to address a partner with a different formulation such as: "Please, can you wait; I still have something else to do," or "Do you think you could tone it down?" or "Next time, you will be more skillful, for sure!"

Partnership means cooperation, and therefore, a child can take over tasks that are truly helpful. For instance, the child can help to carry something in or out, clean up, carefully carry a glass, or quietly close a door. Tests prove how eager two- and three-year-olds are and how sincerely they try to demonstrate their efficiency in providing help.

"You are really a big help to me." Such a statement reinforces self-confidence and also influences a child's social behavior toward others. The willingness to help is often well intended, but a child lacks the proper basic prerequisites that must still be acquired. Adults should make suggestions, such as how one can give a helping hand to another child climbing up a staircase, to assist without irritating, or what speed should be used to push a stroller without worrying a small child, or how a second child can be taken along on a bicycle without both falling off. These contacts start in the first year of life and can be accomplished by simple means—through partnership and cooperation as a part of the socio-emotional experience.

19 Development of Individuality and Self-Confidence. Small Groups and Play Units.

We have already explained earlier why children's early experiences are so dependent upon adjustment to their environment. Self-confidence or distrust, openness or shyness, will determine individual personality. A self-assured attitude helps the child to gain critical objectivity. For instance, children are not easily "lured" into performing tasks that they are unable to do or which they refuse to do.

Children's own willfulness is always a positive beginning in the development of their individuality. This willfulness and self-assurance is often irritating to the world around them. Yet this self-reliance helps children in gaining the insight they need to become independent, namely, understanding the differences among other children, between older or handicapped people, as well as understanding their daily duties that require mutual help and consideration. Movement play and sports offer many possibilities for togetherness, and for personal and joint responsibility. The behavior of parents and teachers influences that of children and may determine their behavior for the rest of their lives.

All children need self-confidence; out of self-confidence grows confidence in others, in partnerships, or in groups. Each child is different—each needs individual, personal attention. It is not necessary for a child to be of the same opinion as another child or to act the same as other children. Therefore, it is very important during movement play to find individual solutions again and again. Individual movement actions are as diverse as children's individual personalities, and these can be reinforced by being recognized. Thus, an individual style of movement is formed.

For children with pronounced individualism, the disciplinary measures imposed in kindergarten or when entering school may represent an impediment to and a suppression of their spontaneity. An educator may be overtaxed when trying to set up well-organized play units in

Who is the stronger? Who can pull the other one off his spot? Even when "working against each other," the task requires cooperation.

overcrowded groups, especially when the educator is hampered by supervisory duties. The adjustment to group play should be an outgrowth of the individual child's independent play.

Small groups may be formed for play around a hoop or a rope placed on the ground, or an "island area" marked with chalk to jointly solve a problem within a group of three or four players. Even if one or more children drop out of their "family" early in play, they will gradually learn to master their tasks within a small unit. A certain color identifying the group or a distinct name for the group will strengthen the feeling of togetherness.

After a while, small groups expand into larger units with about eight to twelve children who will jointly and independently play ball games, jump rope, or work on the horizontal bar.

These play units meeting on playgrounds are often formed on the spur of the moment, and children should not be influenced in selecting their own team. Within these play units such social structures as leader of the game, spectators, willing participants, and willful opponents develop. Negative experiences are necessary, too. However, the more knowledge children acquire about their own limitations, the more they will critically recognize any negative effects at an early stage and will positively use this knowledge to establish their own sense of values.

20 By Playing Together, Parents Achieve a Closer Relationship With Their Children.

More than most other forms of communication, sports and games are suited to be practiced as family activities. Today, more than ever before, parents act as teachers in skiing, swimming, and in playing tennis. In our [Liselott Diem's] swimming classes, it is usually the fathers who create new water games for children in their first year of life, thereby changing their own relationship toward their children.

By playing together with their children, parents can gain contacts hardly ever achieved through talk or other forms of interaction. Playing is always based on spontaneity, on situational perception, and on reaction. Partners need to be patient in practice and while acquiring the necessary playing skills. They learn together with others and from each other.

This communication during play also applies when boys and girls play together. Children should never be forced to play a certain role, and definitely not the traditional roles for girls or boys. The characteristics attributed to the sexes have been shown to be questionable and to hamper individual development. There are no typically male or female characteristics other than varied manifestations of these characteristics in individual human beings. Girls enjoy playing soccer just as much as boys enjoy dancing. Such depends on a child's talent and the contacts an individual child has with other children, as well as on the environment and the social circumstances. Regardless of sex, the individual child should develop his or her personal preferences and hobbies through coeducational upbringing.

This applies especially to games and lifetime sports, the types of sports that can be pursued from early childhood on to late in life, for example, swimming, rowing, ice skating, snow skiing, bicycling, and tennis.

A child's motivation for a certain sports discipline is determined by the sports climate set in the home. When the whole family participates in swimming and skiing, or attends soccer or tennis games together, lasting impressions will be unconsciously formed that will influence the ability to learn and quickly adopt a new sports technique. Whether or not children will later qualify themselves as fencers or gymnasts is not so much a consequence of inherent talent, but rather the result of early ventures and experiences.

Family games begin in the first year of life and develop equally well everywhere—in the house or in the garden, in the street, during leisure time on weekends or during vacation. Typical for family games are the cooperative play of the young and the old, of parents and children, as well as of children of different ages.

The following examples are taken from several resources, including *100 Tips for Leisure Time Fun*, published by the German Federal Department for Youth, Family and Health, and the booklets *Sports for All* and *Get Trim After Work*, published by the German Sports Federation.

Father Becomes a Living Horizontal Bar

The thumbs become the bar, while the father's other fingers clasp around the small wrist. The "gymnasts" better take off their shoes! Now they are going to try to turn a somersault around the "thumb bar." Father's legs and stomach can be of help, too. The children try to climb up using their feet, to push off, and to roll forward through father's arms. Now the tips of the toes search for the ground. Father opens his arms wide so that the "turner" stands up again!

Jumping and Turning

Children are supposed to jump high using four or fewer jumps to move once around a circle.

Joint tasks and shared roles bring children and parents closely together.

The Giant Jump
From a squat position, the child tries to push off strongly, mainly using the big toes in a giant jump way up into the air.

Pilot Jump
Father helps the child to jump really high. While airborne, the father stops the child in mid air. While suspended thusly, the jumper squats or straddles the legs or holds them in a horizontal position! Guess who lasts the longest?

Throwing at a Target
Build a pyramid from cans. The throwers line up at a designated distance and aim at the cans with cloth or tennis balls. Two teams may be formed. The team that knocks down the largest number of cans with its 20 balls is declared the winner. Don't you remember this game?

Boccia and Croquet
Remember the Italian game *Boccia* or the game of croquet with its wickets and wooden mallets? All that's needed are a walkway, a grassy area, or any open space and a few small wooden balls in different colors. The equipment can be home made. Let's start. Throwing, striking, aiming, bending, and lots of laughter. After all, it's just a game.

Rope Jumping
Runners, jumpers, boxers, and weight lifters keep fit through rope jumping. Agility, fast reaction, and good physical condition are necessary to avoid getting tangled up. It works even better when two turn a long jump rope and the jumper has to adjust to an unfamiliar rhythm. You won't believe how agile and yet relaxed one can become.

21 Health Education. Children Are Endurance Achievers. Conditioning of the Body to Withstand Climatic Changes Need Not Be a Tough Task. Hygienic Measures.

Health encompasses the physical, mental, and social well-being of an individual. Any interference in development or behavior turns into system-wide disorder. At the same time, physical weaknesses retard general behavior. Furthermore, emotional impairment such as anxiety and fear affect motor coordination, dexterity, or fast reactions. In early childhood, movement ability is the key to knowledge and behavior in general. Basic practical experiences are mentally stimulating and promote the development of intelligence. Each success or failure contributes to new insights and to sensory-motor perceptions.

Strictly speaking, health education can be summarized in a few key points:
- enhancement of endurance and respiratory efficiency;
- conditioning as a way of adapting and resisting respiratory illnesses;
- versatile muscular effort for holding and explosive power.

The child is an endurance achiever because of the sum total of repeated, short-term physical efforts. The number of rhythmical, singular efforts with changing energy levels often exceeds the endurance level of an adult. A monotonous endurance effort without change of tension will not meet a child's movement needs. Running games such as hide-and-seek, as well as ball games, contain a short-term, high-stress interval, as well as rest periods. During sled riding on a hillside, the repeated up and down activity, which often lasts for hours, is testimony of a child's endurance. This again, in a sense, is interval training, a number of short energy bursts coupled with phases of recovery.

All endurance performances also involve respiratory training and increase breathing capacity. During swimming and diving, a child will instinctively learn how to rhythmically inhale and exhale. Inhaling through the nose is preferred to breathing through the mouth because the air is warmed and cleaned of dust by the sieve-like fine hair in the nostrils. Colds and infections of the nose and throat area can be avoided by breathing through the nose.

Conditioning should not be regarded as a harsh measure, but rather as a way of increasing the adaptability of the body to warm and cold stimuli. Conditioning of the body can already start in the first year of life through short baths at varying temperatures, by using Turkish towels, and through dry brushing of the skin. The child should get used to warm and cold showers in such a way that these changes feel comfortable, and should also practice skin care through running around naked. Warm-up suits prevent the necessary conditioning against temperature changes, and temperature regulation in living rooms and work-out areas eliminates the alternating stimulation provided by variations in temperature. Children regard the changes between a hot sauna and the cold snow as very pleasant if they were exposed to them from early childhood on. Colds result from lack of adaptation to functional changes. Stimulation must be brief to have an intense effect. Children should never shiver or freeze. Short-term exposure to wind and cold stimuli result in invigorated and sensitized epidermal vessels, not only because the skin regulates body temperature, but also because the skin is one of our most important sensory organs. The skin acts as a sensory organ for receiving and guiding, for touching, as an organ for control, communication, and contact. In particular, walking bare foot stimulates the reflex zones in the soles of the feet, which control body alignment.

A child should, at an early stage, get used to daily, thorough cleaning of the entire body—to brushing, massaging, and vigorous drying with a towel. Change of clothing, especially underwear and socks, affects health in the same way as does proper fitting of shoes as far as size, width, and flexibility at the ankles are concerned. While playing, or taking part in any sports, children should wear air permeable clothing. Afterward, they should change their clothing to stay warm. Fatigue and reluctance, along with nervous overexcitement, are the result of incorrect living habits, insufficient oxygen respiration, and shallow breathing. Incorrect nutrition results in just as many irritations as does lack of movement intensity.

22 Good Posture Is Not a Static Concept. Strength and Weakness of the Foot and Back. Control of Everyday Behavior.

"Good posture" is not a static entity and cannot be considered as a static process. Posture is an expression of personality; it changes through the internal and external condition of a human being and is expressed by its movement behavior. An upright posture has to be achieved over and over again. Therefore, it is more appropriate to talk about the *development* of body posture. This evolvement of body posture is a difficult task in human development. It can be systematically developed through suitable positions and movement impulses such as lying in prone position, crawling, and pulling oneself up, to prevent overload. In a fully upright position, the main load is carried by the legs and feet, which often show incorrect weight distribution due to incorrect posture. All weaknesses of the foot can really be avoided.

The foot is a multi-jointed body part that provides cushioning for the human body. It is constructed of several elaborate arches that in turn consist of many little, individual building blocks and joints that are linked together through tendons and muscles. The displacement or collapse of a part of the arch will naturally cause some general changes. This is the reason why we talk about—
- fallen arches, i.e., when the longitudinal arches sink;
- pronation of the foot, i.e., when an internal bend is clearly visible on the Achilles tendon, which protrudes to the inside;
- splay foot, occurring when the metatarsal arch is overly spread.

Any of these weaknesses can be eliminated through specific and intensive strengthening of the supportive muscles. In this regard, a child needs suitable movement games and movement tasks. Most important for foot support is the use of the toe flexors. In order to push off the floor, a child has to learn to use the toes as feelers. Incorrect, rigid shoes and constriction through too tight socks

A child with a firm grip will try to lift the legs backward above the head and squat through. Starting with this simple task, the child moves back and forth. Through this game the abdominal muscles are strengthened.

Moving forward hand over hand in a straight cross-hang is an athletic task. One notices the exertion and concentration by just looking at the "helping" tongue.

force the muscles of the toes to remain inactive, especially those which are responsible for bending and spreading the toes. Thus, muscles remain weak within the "corset" surrounding them. Correct posture can be identified by three main characteristics:
• proper alignment of the feet;
• proper alignment of the pelvis;
• proper alignment of the shoulder girdle and the head.

Alignment depends on the alternation of active and passive stretching of the supportive muscles that surround parts of the bone structure. When a muscle releases its tension, the entire static conditions change. For example, weak abdominal muscles cause a pelvic tilt, a "hollow back" develops, and the supportive ability of the spine thus disturbed shifts its stress to the knees and feet.

The many-membered skeletal supports of the foot and the spine are especially sensitive to postural alignment. By nature they are built for elasticity and flexibility, and the holding and the supporting muscles are constantly in need of stress and strengthening. However, constant stress in the form of static standing or sitting will cause damage.

A partial postural weakness is always part of a system-wide weakness. We differentiate between:
• heart-circulatory-respiratory weakness;
• muscular weaknesses;
• poor coordination.

In addition to the already described weaknesses of the foot, weaknesses of the trunk, which are related to curvature of the spine, can be easily and graphically recognized. The normal, S-shaped curvature loses its elasticity when the curvatures in the upper, lower, or both sections have developed to the extreme, or when the curvature is missing completely. Here, we are talking about:
• kyphosis, i.e., when the thoracic region of the spine is excessively rounded;
• lordosis, i.e., when the lumbar region is excessively curved forward;
• the hollow, round back, a combination of kyphosis and lordosis;
• the flat back, where the curvatures are missing.
Strengthening of the long back stretchers (trapezius and latissimus dorsi muscles) occurs through hanging and swinging exercises, while climbing, pullovers, and casting off strengthen the muscles of the entire torso.

Flexibility of the spine can be controlled and practiced through loose, wave-like movements, bending and stretching in alternation with turning, and with sideward and backward movements.

Learning to hang and swing with a sure grip, as well as to climb and to support, is possible on horizontal bars. Children mastering these tasks possess strength in the torso and, consequently, postural strength.

The control of daily behavior is even more important than appropriate, compensating exercises. Children should relax as often as possible through reading or playing while lying in a prone position. Children often choose to sit in tailor fashion, for instance, on a chair; this is a natural and healthy sitting posture. Like older people, children should move a lot; they should run and skip and never stand still for long periods of time. Standing is tiring for the supportive muscles of the foot, as well as those of the spine, because the resulting pressure acts on the sensitive discs between the vertebrae. These can only refill their liquid centers through relief of tension.

The embodiment of a weak, uncoordinated, stiff, and tense child is one who possesses postural weakness and lack of movement. Both can be eliminated through corrective measures.

23 Endurance and Speed.

Toddlers are endurance achievers. The sum total of their movement achievements often exceeds the endurance performance of an adult. However, these achievements are not reached uniformly, but rather irregularly through the dynamics of speed and the extension of strength. The child moves with alternating speeds, sometimes faster, sometimes slower. Muscle contractions alternate between dynamic strength and recovery. Herein concealed is the secret of interval training as a natural course that results in endurance. Endurance is limited by muscle fatigue; this exhaustion is the result of the pumping effort by the heart to sustain circulation and metabolism. The greater the pumping intensity of the heart and the capacity of the lungs in supplying oxygen, the better the muscles will work, especially if their elasticity is capable of removing bodily waste and toxins.

In the first year of life, a child already needs movement performance objectives that can be achieved with alternating efforts, namely, strong pushing, pressing, kicking, lifting, and holding, as well as releasing, shaking, and relaxing. Already in the first year of life, a child can swim with great perseverance and self-motivation. We limit these movement performances to 20 to 30 minutes and can tell from the protests of the children when we ask them to get out of the water that they are motivated and not only are devoted to playing in the water, but feel comfortable in it.

Endurance performances should be selected according to children's ages and desires. Sports that consist of the natural alternation between stress and relief, and promote endurance, are typical sports activities for children, for instance: riding a scooter, snow skiing, ice skating, and ball play. Although rest periods are injected from time to time, the total efforts often last one to two hours.

According to standardized tests, running performances without rest intervals should last no longer than four minutes for six-year-olds and six minutes for eight-year-olds. However, these numbers should be considered minimum achievements. During community sports festival competitions, one can observe many examples of eight-year-olds

Running games promote speed and endurance. In this picture, the children are trying to skillfully throw their balls into the bucket.

running distances of five to six miles. The driving forces in these efforts are usually community, family, and friends, and the running tempo is usually moderate. It is not the distance that "kills," but rather the speed. This is one of the oldest rules of training.

Endurance produces resistance against fatigue. One who trains the circulatory and metabolic systems on a regular basis will tire less easily and can perform with better intelligence, as well as elevating his or her concentration.

Speed is dependent on fast reaction and coordination. Children learn to recognize situations and to react quickly through many different experiences. Nowadays, children often adjust to traffic situations far better than adults. They react automatically to familiar situations, and the daily use of movement and orientation training helps them avoid accidents.

In order to fully develop speed and reaction ability, a child needs open spaces, not confined areas. The child needs spacious grounds upon which to run, race, chase, run in curves, or quickly change direction. Fast reaction can also be improved through trampolining, ball games, and especially through table tennis with its fast bouncing small ball. Children are provided many opportunities for play and are good students due to imitating and practicing on their own. All they need is encouragement and open playing areas. Prohibitive rules and hindrances impair the teaching of any kind of children's games that promote endurance and speed.

Children love to run short distances; they repeat these runs many times, similar to interval training. Thus they build up their endurance.

Games using jumping skills promote quickness. Large cans are set up close together so that jumping most likely can continue without a break.

24 Strength, Flexibility, and Skillfulness.

Children develop strength by managing their own body weight. Muscles are strengthened through any kind of action in which children pull themselves up, climb, mount bars, perform cartwheels, or support themselves. In movement actions, strength can be displayed in the form of take-off power, lifting power, as supportive hold, and as a driving force or a holding force. Consequently, strength is a static as well as a dynamic effort. Dynamic strength is essential for children when applied within movement actions, for instance, in the take-off, while mounting, and when climbing. Children who hang, swing, climb, pull, and support themselves a great deal do not have postural weaknesses. A well-developed muscular system can be recognized by its profile (muscle tone) as well as its blood circulation. The chemically refined metabolic process of supplying oxygen and discarding carbon dioxide, and the exchange processes within muscles, are triggered only through constant use of the organic movement systems. The more differentiated children develop their movement skills, the better they will develop their body condition, fitness, and, consequently, their overall condition.

Strength can be defined as either explosive power or as stamina. During the performance of jumping or when starting to run, resistance has to be overcome by applying maximum muscle contraction in the shortest time, i.e., with maximum speed and explosive power. During uphill bicycling or while mountain climbing, strength has to be applied over extended periods of time.

Muscle tone is the state of tension in a muscle. This is visible through the shape assumed by the muscle. Muscle tone depends on the stretchability of the muscle (similar to the drawn string of a bow). Therefore, control of the mobility of the joints is an important prerequisite for strength. Children who always lean forward while sitting, writing, or reading—perhaps because they can't see very well or because of bad lighting—shorten the anterior muscles of the torso, avoid a total stretch of the upper spine, and prevent the back stretchers (trapezius and latissimus dorsi muscles) from being put to full use. Elasticity of the muscles and stretchability through extensive flexibility are

Children should learn to take care of their own safety. Climbing across stairs made from old railroad ties proves it.

as equally important for achieving full strength as muscle tension and contraction. Hypertension of the muscles causes cramping while lack of tension results in slackness. Children's external appearance is always closely related to their mental-emotional condition.

We have repeatedly described the importance of coordination, but we want to point out once more an existing interrelationship; skillfulness is the result of good coordination. Coordination can be disturbed or inhibited by a lack of strength or flexibility. Muscular weakness and awkwardness can curtail the joy of movement and the feeling of achievement. The same applies to children's endurance and ability to concentrate. Children need equipment for playing and playmates to stimulate their ability to excel and to bring forth enjoyment with maximum effort.

Most children suffer more from under- rather than overtaxing of their movement skills.

Group pulling games are as important in judo as in tug-of-war.

25 Properly Planned Play Areas in the Home, Near the Home, and on the Playground.

More space for open play—let's give some thought to this consideration. In doing so, one has to think about:
• the playing area in the home;
• the playing area near the home;
• the playing area on the playground.

At home or in the house, a toddler needs opportunities for crawling, walking, climbing, balancing, hanging, and swinging, as well as for playing with balloons, larger and smaller balls, and jump ropes, not to mention space for rolling and turning cartwheels.

Architects provide examples of how to create a room divider in the form of a trellis, which serves as a climbing wall. A foam mattress can be used for tumbling, rolling, and jumping and as a trampoline for basic forms of bouncing, including turns, seat drops, and front drops.

A play corner should be designated, equipped with blackboards for drawing or for target games with balls. Such an area should contain changeable apparatus that permits activities which combine balancing and climbing. The objects children should be able to handle on their own should be colorful and require little maintenance, and as such, they become part of the living area.

Playing areas near the house—in the backyard or in a courtyard—were hardly ever given consideration in the past. As such, the wall of a house could be prepared for play in the same way as different floor surfaces. Some of the games children play—marbles, hopscotch, and riding a scooter—work better on an asphalt surface and on hard, even ground. Other games develop only in areas with hiding places, thickets, and play corners. Therefore, it is important to carefully subdivide and landscape the area around the home to provide an incentive for play. A hill or a wide staircase with a sandy area in front suitable for jumping are two such examples. Another would be an even surface area, ideal for basketball games where hoops are attached to a wall or a mini-game soccer goal.

Playgrounds with suitable play equipment should be available near the home.

In playing areas on a playground, it is necessary that many different opportunities for play are coordinated with each other. The play areas should be usable in a variety of ways; this applies to the ground, the walls, the corners, and the edges.

Areas with a flat and hard playing surface can be marked with different colors for hopscotch or ball games. They may also be equipped with embedded receptacles for goal posts, baskets, and nets. The latter can be stored in weather-resistant storage sheds. Hard surfaces are ideally suited for riding a scooter and bicycling, for bowling and other ball-rolling games, or for jumping rope.

Sandy surfaces surrounded by landings or steps that can serve as jumping off spots are also ideal. These can be used to mark standing broad jump distances. High bars and swings can also be located in this area.

Grassy areas suited for running and peg games, which are not adversely affected by uneven surfaces, are also important for children. These green areas may be subdivided into smaller units for group games using suitable planting arrangements.

Wall areas must be planned on a more generous scale. They should be easy to maintain and be appropriately marked net-high for practicing tennis strokes, with an outline of a soccer goal, or with square or round colored targets for various types of ball games.

Why shouldn't climbing hooks and fixed ropes be installed in a wall that would *invite* "mountain climbing?" Steep, artificially-created slopes provide opportunities for pulling up, climbing, mounting, or sliding down a smooth chute.

Even inside the home, a beach ball suspended from the ceiling leads to a diversified game.

Playground in a housing complex.

Steps arranged at different elevations encourage playing much more than do level areas.

Subdivisions of the play areas and the creation of different elevations are greater incentives for play than are large, stark, smooth, and empty areas. Traditional ball games must also be promoted as mini-games such as mini-soccer, mini-basketball, mini-hockey, and mini-tennis. These encourage imaginative ideas involving novel combinations, new equipment, and self-invented rules. Safety factors should not necessarily rule out all elements of risk, because without risk there is no adventure, and without uncertainty of outcome there is no game. Playgrounds that have been correctly designed will open up versatile, independent actions, partnerships, and social experiences for the child.

Complex and comprehensive actions develop through this type of tandem swinging on a wobbly tire.

26 Appropriate Play Equipment.

Different types of play equipment for various movement activities should offer the child diversified stimulation. This means play equipment that is neither too plentiful nor too one-sided.

For tests of balance, we always select balls and equipment that are different in weight and form and different in resilience and elasticity.

What follows is a list of basic play equipment types that can be purchased from specialty dealers and in department stores.

Small Equipment and Hand Implements

Balls
- Playground balls, multicolor, and in different sizes
- Throwing balls in different sizes
- Push balls, flyweight balls
- Medicine balls
- Beach balls
- Soccer balls, handballs, basketballs, volleyballs, Japan balls

Balloons
Table tennis balls and racquets
Shuttlecocks and badminton racquets
Wands
Hoops
Jump ropes, long ropes (double dutch ropes), chinese jump ropes
Magic ropes, tug-of-war ropes
"Knips" ball game
"Indiaca" ball game
Ring toss game
Hoppity hop ball
Roller skates
Scooters
Bicycles
Pedal cars, go carts, kitt cars

Mini-games
    Croquet
    Bocce (boccia)
    Mini-tennis
    Mini-golf
    Mini-hockey
    Mini-soccer
    Mini-handball
    Mini-volleyball

Movable Equipment

Round beam with ladder and sliding board
"Junior-Sport-Combi" set with ladder and sliding board
Small vaulting box
Take-off trampoline
Mini-trampoline
Moving balancing beam
Mats

Indoor Play Equipment

Door chinning bar
Climbing wall with climbing ropes and horizontal bar
    elements
Stall bars
Climbing ropes
Basketball hoops
Soccer goals

Built-in Equipment

Horizontal bar for children, height: 35 inches
Horizontal bar for children, height: 47 inches
Horizontal bar for children, height: 59 inches
Swing
Climbing trestle tree apparatus
Balance beam

27 Tests and Self-Evaluation of Movement Performance. 0–5 Years.

First Contacts with the Environment

Brief lifting of the head from a prone position
Step-like movements when the child is held in an upright position
Clasping and gripping with fingers when the inside of palms are touched
Clasping and gripping with toes when the sole of the foot is touched

First Movement Achievements

Pushing and Supporting Abilities

4–6 Months
Longer periods of unaided lifting of the head from a prone position while propping up with hands
From prone position pushing off strongly with the feet against a supporting hand
From prone position with knees drawn under the stomach pushing-off strongly from a mat using the toes
Unrestrained crawling

6–12 Months
Turning onto the stomach or back without any outside help
Crawling and pulling up onto the knees using a support
Pulling up to a straight back sitting position
Crawling up steps and standing up
First aided steps

Eye-Hand Coordination

4–12 Months
Touching, pressing, crumbling, getting hold of materials
Chasing and independently directing a moving object (ball)
Making sounds with rattles and clappers

Expanding Conceptual Domains

Perception of Equilibrium

1–3 Years
Sitting, standing, kneeling
Walking with and without help
Standing and walking on tip-toes
Rocking, feathering, and bouncing on a mattress or on a trampoline

Orientation in Space

Running up and down (a hill)
Climbing up, down, and over
Rolling and turning

Development of Capabilities and Skills in Partner and Group Relationships

Ability to Run and Jump, Ability to Support

3 Years
Rocking, feathering, jumping (with both feet, with one foot)
Climbing, hand-over-hand climbing, hanging, swinging
Handstand, headstand, and shoulderstand with spotting
Carrying, pulling, pushing, pressing
Standing long jump, standing high jump
Crawling and climbing around, over, and through obstacles

4–5 Years
Running and skipping with changes in speed and direction
Skipping games, jumping rope

Climbing up and down trees, ladders, and climbing equipment
Handstand, headstand, shoulderstand, and cartwheel with free movement transitions
Pushing, pressing, pulling, and carrying of a partner, unaided moving of equipment
Running long jump, running high jump, jumping over obstacles

Balance, Coordination

3 Years
Balancing on stationary and moving equipment
Feathering, bouncing, and jumping on the trampoline
Riding a scooter, riding a bicycle (with training wheels)

4–5 Years
Balancing on stationary and moving equipment with additional tasks
Riding a scooter, bicycling, roller skating
Walking on stilts
Snow skiing, ice skating, sled riding

Skillfulness, Reaction

3 Years
Throwing, catching, and rolling a ball
Hitting with hands or heading a light ball in upward motion
Playing ball games with adults
Juggling of objects using different body parts

4–5 Years
Hitting, heading, kicking, and bouncing a ball
Throwing and rolling at a target
Games with a hoop, a rope, "Knipsball," Indiaca
Climbing, ascending, jumping, balancing, and running in a variety of ways
Movement combinations

Endurance

3 Years
Running (3–5 minutes)

4–5 Years
Running (5–7 minutes)

Speed

3 Years
Running races (dashes of 15–20 meters)
Racing with adults

4–5 Years
Short distance races of 20–40 meters
Running in competition, relay races, slalom runs, obstacle courses
Simple games involving running and catching

Communication and Situational Orientation

Running in pairs and groups, chasing, and catching
Dodging and meeting partners
Ball games with a partner
Rope jumping
Play within a group—open play and games with rules
Setting up equipment with others
Spotting a partner for safety

28 Tests and Self-Evaluation—Examples for 6–8 Years.

Balance/Coordination

Riding a scooter, roller skating, bicycling
 Change of direction and speed, meeting others and dodging, stopping, starting, moving in slalom fashion, partner exercises.

Ice skating, snow skiing, sled riding

Balancing on stationary equipment (round beam, balance beam)
 Walking forward and backward, running, skipping, turning, changing direction, meeting, dodging, stepping over obstacles, balancing with additional tasks, such as ball throwing and catching.

Balancing on moving equipment (thick rope, rope ladder, wobble beam, balance disk, medicine ball)
 Walking forward and backward, running, standing on one leg, sitting, kneeling, turning, wobbling, balancing with additional tasks, such as carrying something and juggling.

Upsetting balance
 Pulling and pushing a partner, pushing off a partner.

Skillfulness
 Juggling with objects in the hands, on the head, headstand, handstand, shoulderstand, cartwheel, walking on stilts.

Equilibrium in the water
 Balancing and rowing, paddling with the hands while floating on an air mattress or on a raft, paddling, canoeing.

Horseback riding
Control of body posture, juggling with balls, horseback riding while standing up in the stirrups.

Reaction/Speed/Skillfulness

Ball games/free exploration
with balloons, Japan balls, beach balls, volley balls, soccer balls, playground balls; rolling, throwing, heading, kicking of the ball, playing ball against a wall; heading the ball while jumping up; dribbling, kicking for distance, dodging, playing around a partner; getting the ball into the goal, a net or a basket; passing or catching a ball while running; obstacle-slalom runs with a ball.

Playing against opponents and blocking

Games with rules
Mini-soccer, mini-basketball, mini-volleyball, mini-handball, mini-hockey, mini-tennis, table tennis: learning and practicing of fundamental techniques, play tactics and procedures, playing games by the rules.

Games involving catching, competitive running games, circle games, fast reaction games
Jumping rope, games with wands, rubber twist games (Chinese jump ropes).

Endurance and Strength: Muscular and Endurance Strength for Holding and Supporting the Body

Force against resistance
Tug-of-war, pulling or pushing a partner out of a circle; pulling, pushing, or carrying of equipment.

Judo, disturbance of equilibrium, winning through submission
Shoulder, hip, foot or leg throws, techniques for breaking falls, falling exercises, grappling, lever techniques on the floor.

Teeter-tottering, hanging, swinging
    Hanging on ropes, swinging, long hanging, inverted hang, skin the cat on still rings, on flying rings; swinging, swinging with a half turn over an obstacle timing the release for controlled landing; swinging on climbing poles; pendulum swinging.

Climbing, ascending, pulling up
    Climbing on climbing towers, cargo nets, climbing trees, and moving equipment; climbing up and over equipment and dismounting.

Cartwheels, handstands, handsprings

Speed/Explosive Power

Long jump, high jump, vaulting
    Rear scissors vault, squat, straddle, flank vault.

Horizontal bar exercises
    Hip pullover forward and backward, front and back hip circles, mounts and dismounts.